OVER 150 OF THE WORLD'S FAMOUS TROPICAL DRINK RECIPES

DON'T STOP THE
TROPICAL DRINKS

W9-DCI-538

GLASSES TO USE FOR DIFFERENT TYPES OF DRINKS

- **14 oz Collins Glass**
  - Soft Drinks
  - Alcoholic Juice Drinks
  - Collins
  - Sours
  - Bloody Mary
- **8 oz Highball**
  - Bourbon/Ginger
  - White Russian
- **4½ oz Rocks**
  - Chilled Shooters
  - Single Shots
- **6 oz Cocktail Glass**
  - Martinis
  - Any chilled "up" drinks
- **8 oz Wine Glass**
  - Wine
  - Champagne

- **2 oz Sherry Glass**
  - Liqueurs
  - Layered Shooters
  - Ports
- **17½ oz Snifter**
  - Brandies
  - Cognacs
- **8½ oz Footed Mug**
  - All Hot Drinks

Always pour light liquors before any liqueurs. Liqueurs are heavier causing the flavor to possibly adhere to the jigger. When pouring numerous drinks, line the glasses up collectively and hold the jigger by the rear of the glass. This allows you to move more quickly and to have better control of the bottle. Always rinse a jigger after using a liqueur. Place the jigger on its side after use in order to allow any excess to drain. When possible, acquire a spill mat: this is a necessity for serious bartenders.

Tulip

Cocktail Glass

Shooter

Irish Coffee Mug

Cordial

Champagne Flute

Wine Goblet

Rocks/ Old Fashion

Sherry Glass

Highball Glass

Snifter

Beer Mug

Punch Cup

Daiquiri

Margarita

Martini

Pony

Hurricane

Champagne Saucer

Parfait Glass

Collins

3

BOTTLE SIZES

Miniature	50 ml	1.7 oz.
Split	187 ml	6.3 oz.
½ Pint	200 ml	6.8 oz.
Tenth	375 ml	12.7 oz.
Pint	500 ml	16.9 oz.
Fifth	750 ml	25.4 oz.
Quart	1 liter	33.8 oz.
Magnum	1.5 L	50.7 oz.
Half Gallon	1.75 L	59.2 oz.
Jeroboam	3 liters	101.4 oz.

MEASUREMENTS

1 Dash	1/32 oz.
1 Teaspoon	1/8 oz.
1 Tablespoon	3/8 oz/
1 Pony	1 oz.
1 Jigger	11/2 oz.
1 Wine Glass	4 oz.
1 Split	6 oz.
1 Cup	8 oz.

STANDARD BAR MEASUREMENTS

Measurements	Metric Equivalent	Standard Equivalent
1 dash	0.9 ml	1/32 oz.
1 teaspoon	3.7 ml	1/8 oz.
1 tablespoon	11.1 ml	3/8 oz.
1 pony	29.5 ml	1 oz.
1 jigger	44.5 ml	1½ oz.
1 miniature	59.2 ml	2 oz.
1 wine glass	119.0 ml	4 oz.
1 split	177.0 ml	6 oz.
1 half pint	257.0 ml	8 oz.
1 tenth	378.88 ml	12.8 oz.
1 "pint" (½ bottle wine)	375.2 ml	12 oz.
1 pint	472.0 ml	16 oz.

4

DRINK CHART

Body Weight	1	2	3	4	5	6
100	.038	.075	.113	.150	.188	.225
120	.031	.063	.094	.125	.156	.188
140	.027	.054	.080	.107	.134	.161
160	.023	.047	.070	.094	.17	.141
180	.021	.042	.063	.083	.104	.124
200	.019	.038	.056	.075	.094	.13
220	.017	.034	.051	.068	.085	.102
240	.016	.031	.047	.063	.078	.094

Impaired DO NOT DRIVE	Intoxicated DO NOT DRIVE

This is a guide only. Food consumption, medication and other physical conditions may vary these figures.

One drink is one shot of 80 proof liquor, 12 oz. beer, or 4 oz. wine

5

HOW TO STOCK A BAR

- **Spirits**
  Brandy
  Gin
  White or Gold Rum
  Dark Rum
  Tequila
  Vodka *(unflavored)*
  Flavored Vodka *(orange, lemon, raspberry, etc.)*
  Bourbon Whiskey
  Tennessee Whiskey
  Single Malt Whiskey
  Irish Whiskey

- **Liqueur**
  Triple Sec or Cointreau
  Apple Pucker Schnapps
  (for Appletinis)
  Kahlua
  Irish Cream
  Southern Comfort
  Amaretto

- **Mixers**
  Sweet & Sour
  Lime Juice *(Fresh or Roses)*
  Bloody Mary Mix
  Margarita Mix
  Fresh Juices *(orange, cranberry, pineapple, pomegranate)*
  Club Soda
  Tonic
  Ginger Ale
  Cola
  Grenadine
  Cream or Half & Half

- **Garnishes**
  Lime Wedges
  Lemon Wedges
  Orange Slices
  Maraschino Cherries
  Olives *(regular or stuffed)*
  Cocktails Onions
  Margarita Salt
  Sugar

- **Wine and Fortified Wines**
  Dry Vermouth
  Sweet Vermouth
  Red Wine
  (Cabernet, Merlot, etc.)
  White Wine *(Chardonnay, Sauvignon Blanc, etc.)*
  Sparkling Wine
  (Champagne, Prosecco, etc.

- **Bitters**
  Angostura Bitters
  Campari

BRANDY

Brandy is a spirit made from distilled grape wine, containing 40-60% ethyl alcohol by volume. This spirit is also made from grape pomace, fermented fruit juice or other fruits such as apples or cherries. Caramel coloring is added to imitate the aging in wooden casks, pomace and fruit brandies are generally not aged and clear in color. Brandy is a very popular after dinner drink. The unique fruity flavoring of brandy makes a great cocktail base. Seventy five percent of Brandy sold in the US comes from California. Brandy is made all over the world, the most famous coming from the Cognac Region of France.

Cognac named after the town of Cognac in France is a brandy produced in this region. The grapes used must be at least 90% Ugni Blanc, Folle Blanche or Colombard. Most cognac is made from Ugni Blanc grapes only. In order to be called cognac, it must be distilled twice in copper pot stills and aged at least 2 years in French oak barrels.

Brandy Alexander, Pisco Sour and Zombie are some of the most popular mixed drinks prepared with brandy.

7

ALABAZAM

2 oz. brandy
¾ oz. lemon juice
½ oz. Orange Curaçao

½ oz. simple syrup
2 dashes orange bitters
2 oz. soda water

Pour the brandy, lemon juice, Orange Curaçao, simple syrup and orange bitters into a cocktail shaker filled with ice. Shake well. Strain into a highball glass filled with ice. Top with soda water.

AMBROSIA

1 oz. Apple Jack
1 oz. brandy
¼ oz. Cointreau

1 tsp. lemon juice
champagne to fill

Shake the first four ingredients over ice and strain into a champagne flute. Fill with champagne.

APRICOT LADY

1 oz. apricot brandy
1½ oz. light rum
½ tsp. Blue Curaçao

1 tsp. lime juice
1 egg white*
orange wedge

Combine with ice and shake. Strain over crushed ice. Garnish with orange wedge.

* Please use caution when using raw eggs as it may cause certain illnesses.

B&B

1 oz. Benedictine   1 oz. brandy

Pour the Benedictine into a snifter.
Use the back of a bar spoon to gently float the brandy on top.

BAYBERRY PUNCH

2 quarts brandy   16 oz. tea
8 oz. Blue Curaçao   6 oranges
12 lemons   6 oz. grenadine
10 oz. powdered sugar

Slice fruit. Combine the ingredients and mix.
Add ice chunks before serving. Serves 8.

BERMUDA BOUQUET

1 oz. apricot brandy   ½ tsp. grenadine
½ tsp. Blue Curaçao   1 tsp. powdered sugar
1½ oz. dry gin   orange twist

Combine with ice and shake. Strain and add ice.
Garnish with orange twist.

BETWEEN THE SHEETS

¾ oz. brandy
¾ oz. light rum
¾ oz. triple sec

½ oz. lemon juice
lemon twist

Pour the ingredients into a cocktail shaker with ice cubes. Shake well.
Strain into a chilled cocktail glass. Garnish with lemon twist.

BLACKBERRY FIZZ

1 oz. blackberry brandy
3 oz. orange juice
3 oz. sour mix

¼ oz. lemon-lime soda
orange wedge

Combine with ice and stir. Garnish with orange wedge.

BLOOD AND SAND

1 oz. cherry brandy
1 oz. Scotch

1 oz. sweet vermouth
1 oz. orange juice

Combine with ice and shake. Strain and add ice.

BOAT COCKTAIL

½ oz. brandy   1¼ oz. orange juice
1¼ oz. vodka

*Combine vodka and orange juice with ice and shake.
Strain into cocktail glass. Use the back of a bar spoon
to gently float the brandy on top.*

BRANDED BANANA

1½ oz. brandy   2 tsp. lemon juice
1 oz. banana liqueur   lemon slice
splash club soda

*Combine all but soda with ice and shake. Strain and add soda and ice.
Garnish with lemon.*

BRANDED MOCHA PUNCH

1 oz. brandy   dash whipped cream
1 quart coffee   6 chocolate chips
1 quart hot chocolate   1 dash cinnamon

*Combine coffee, hot chocolate and brandy. Garnish with whipped
cream, chocolate chips and cinnamon. Serve hot.*

BRANDY ALEXANDER

1 oz. brandy
1 oz. cream

1 oz. dark crème de cacao
dash ground nutmeg

*Pour the ingredients into a cocktail shaker with ice cubes. Shake well.
Strain into a chilled cocktail glass. Garnish with a dusting of nutmeg.*

BRANDY BOAT

2 oz. brandy
1 dash rum
½ oz. club soda
1 tsp. lemon juice
1 tsp. pineapple juice

2 tsp. sugar syrup
dash lime juice
lemon slice
orange slice

*Combine all but rum and soda with ice and shake. Strain and add
soda and crushed ice. Float Rum on top. Garnish with fruit.*

BRANDY EGGNOG

1¼ oz. milk
1 oz. brandy

½ oz. sugar syrup
1 egg yolk*

*Pour the milk, brandy, sugar syrup and egg yolk into a cocktail shaker
with ice cubes. Shake well. Strain into an old-fashioned glass.*

*Please use caution when using raw eggs as it may cause certain illnesses.

BRANDY MANHATTAN

1½ oz. brandy
½ oz. sweet vermouth

1 maraschino cherry

*Combine with ice and stir. Strain and serve straight up.
Garnish with maraschino cherry.*

BULL'S MILK

1½ oz. brandy
1 oz. rum
8 oz. milk

1 tsp. powdered sugar
dash nutmeg
dash cinnamon

*Combine with ice and shake. Strain and add ice.
Dust with cinnamon and nutmeg.*

CAFÉ GROG

1 oz. brandy
2 oz. spiced rum
4 oz. coffee

1 tsp. sugar
lemon twist

*Combine liqueurs with hot coffee and stir. Add sugar as needed.
Garnish with lemon twist.*

CARDINAL PUNCH

16 oz. brandy
1 bottle claret
1 bottle champagne
8 oz. sweet vermouth
16 oz. white rum

32 oz. club soda
dash powdered sugar
orange slices
lemon slices
lime slices

Combine with ice and stir. Garnish with fruits. Serves 8.

CLARET PUNCH

8 oz. brandy
8 oz. Blue Curaçao
3 quarts claret
1 quart club soda

3 cups lemon juice
1 cup powdered sugar
8 orange slices

Dissolve sugar in lemon juice. Add liqueurs and soda.
Stir and add ice. Garnish with orange slices. Serves 8.

CLASSIC

1 oz. brandy
½ oz. Maraschino
½ oz. triple sec

1½ oz. sour mix
lime twist

Combine with ice and shake. Strain and serve straight up.
Garnish with lime wedge.

COFFEE COCKTAIL

1½ oz. apple brandy
1½ oz. port
1 oz. coffee

1 egg yolk*
dash nutmeg

Combine with ice and shake. Strain and add ice. Top with nutmeg.
Please use caution when using raw eggs as it may cause certain illnesses.

CORPSE REVIVER

¾ oz. apple brandy
¾ oz. Cognac or brandy

½ oz. sweet vermouth

Pour the ingredients into a cocktail shaker with ice. Stir well.
Strain into a chilled cocktail glass.

DEAUVILLE COCKTAIL

½ oz. brandy
½ oz. apple brandy

½ oz. triple sec
½ oz. lemon juice

Shake over ice. Strain into chilled cocktail glass.

EAST INDIA COCKTAIL

1½ oz. cognac
½ oz. Blue Curaçao or Triple Sec

dash orange bitters
1 oz. pineapple juice

Shake with ice. Strain into chilled cocktail glass.

GOLDEN DAWN

1 oz. apple brandy
1 oz. apricot brandy
1 oz. dry gin

1 dash grenadine
2 dashes orange juice

*Combine all but grenadine with ice.
Shake, strain, add ice and grenadine.*

HEAD WIND

1 oz. brandy
1 oz. 151 rum
½ oz. Blue Curaçao
1 oz. dark rum
1 oz. light rum

1 oz. vodka
2 oz. sour mix
4 oz. orange juice
2 oz. pineapple juice
1 slice pineapple

Combine with ice and shake. Strain and add ice. Garnish with fruit.

LA HABANA

1 oz. apricot brandy   juice of half a lime
1 oz. gin

Pour the gin and apricot brandy into a cocktail shaker with ice cubes.
Add a few drops of lime juice. Shake well. Strain into a chilled
cocktail glass three-quarters full of ice.

METROPOLITAN

1½ oz. brandy   ½ tsp. sugar syrup
1 oz. sweet vermouth   2 dashes orange bitters

Pour brandy, sweet vermouth, simple sugar and orange bitters into a
shaker with ice cubes. Shake well. Strain into a chilled cocktail glass.

PISCO SOUR

2 oz. Pisco   dash bitters
lemon juice   1 egg white
sugar to taste

Blend the egg white and sugar in a blender, then add Pisco, lime juice,
ice and bitters. Pour into cocktail glass.

TOM AND JERRY

1 oz. Cognac or brandy   hot milk
1 oz. dark rum   dash grated nutmeg
1 egg*   ½ oz. simple syrup or 1 tsp. powdered sugar

*Separate the egg white from the egg yolk and beat them separately. Fold the
beaten eggs together and place into an Irish coffee mug. Add the sugar or
simple syrup, rum and brandy. Fill with hot milk. Stir well.
Garnish with grated nutmeg.*

*Please use caution when using raw eggs as it may cause certain illnesses.

YELLOW PARROT

¾ oz. apricot brandy   ¾ oz. Yellow Chartreuse
¾ oz. anisette

Stir with ice. Strain into chilled cocktail glass.

ZOMBIE

1¼ oz. lemon juice   ½ oz. light rum
1 oz. dark rum   ½ oz. high-proof dark rum
¾ oz. orange juice   2 dashes grenadine
½ oz. cherry brandy

*Pour the ingredients into a cocktail shaker with ice. Shake well.
Strain into a highball glass with crushed ice.*

Gin

Gin adds a light flavoring to many favorite cocktails. One of the first recipes any bartender needs to learn is the classic martini. While the traditional way to mix a Martini is to stir the ingredients in a mixing glass, many people prefer their's shaken instead, so it is a good idea to ask "Shaken or Stirred?"

Distilled gin is made by redistilling white grain spirit flavored with juniper berries.

Compound gin is produced by flavouring neutral grain spirit with juniper berries without redistilling and is considered a flavoured vodka.

London dry gin is the most common style of gin used for mixed drinks. It is made by using a neutral grain spirit (usually produced in a column still) and redistilling after the botanicals are added. Botanicals like cassia bark, cinnamon, coriander, cardamom, orris (iris) root, angelica root and seed, licorice root, lemon and bitter orange peel, fennel and anise give gin its distinctive character.

Some of the great recipes of time are made with gin, including Martinis, Long Island Iced Teas, Tom Collins. Gin Fizz, Gin and Tonic and the classic Martini are very popular drinks made with gin.

A-BOMB

1½ oz. gin
1 oz. Benedictine

1 splash Blue Curaçao

Build over ice in an old fashioned glass.

ADMIRAL COCKTAIL

2 oz. gin
¾ oz. lime juice

½ oz. Peter Heering

Mix with cracked ice in a shaker.
Strain into chilled cocktail glass.

ALEXANDER COCKTAIL

1 oz. gin
1 oz. white crème de cacao

1 oz. cream
sprinkle nutmeg

Shake with ice and strain into chilled cocktail glass.
Garnish with a sprinkle of nutmeg.

ANGLER'S COCKTAIL

1½ oz. dry gin   2 dashes bitters
1 dash grenadine   2 dashes orange bitters

Combine with ice and shake. Strain and add ice.

APPLE MARTINI

2 oz. gin   apple slice
1 oz. green-apple schnapps

Pour the ingredients into a shaker with ice cubes. Shake well.
Strain into a chilled cocktail glass. Garnish with apple slice.

ARUBA

1½ oz. gin   ½ egg white*
½ oz. White Curaçao   1 tsp. Orgeat Syrup
1 oz. lemon juice   lime wedge

Mix with ice in shaker. Strain into cocktail glass.
Garnish with lime wedge.

*Please use caution when using raw eggs as it may cause certain illnesses.

BERMUDA ROSE COCKTAIL

1½ oz. gin
dash apricot brandy

dash grenadine

Shake and strain into cocktail glass.

BIRD OF PARADISE

2 oz. gin
splash club soda
1 egg white*

1 tsp. grenadine
2 Tbsp. lemon juice
1 tsp. powdered sugar

Combine all but soda with ice and shake. Strain and add ice.
*Please use caution when using raw eggs as it may cause certain illnesses.

BISHOP'S COCKTAIL

1½ oz. gin

1½ oz. ginger wine

Combine with ice and shake. Strain and serve straight up.

BITTER LEMON COOLER

1½ oz. dry gin   dash lemon-lime soda
1½ oz. dry vermouth   1 tsp. raspberry syrup
1 tsp. lemon juice   1 lemon twist

Combine all but soda with ice and shake. Strain and add soda
and ice. Garnish with lemon twist.

BLACK-OUT SHOOTER

½ oz. gin   splash lime juice
½ oz. blackberry brandy

Combine with ice and shake. Strain and serve straight up.

BLOOD HOUND

1½ oz. gin   3-4 strawberries
½ oz. dry vermouth   dash schnapps
½ oz. sweet vermouth   3 oz. ice

Combine with crushed ice and blend until smooth.

BLUE DEVIL

½ oz. Blue Curaçao   1½ oz. sour mix
1 oz. gin

Combine with ice and shake. Strain and serve straight up.

BLUE MOON

1½ oz. gin   2 dashes orange bitters
3 oz. Crème Yvette   orange slice
¾ oz. dry vermouth

Combine with ice and shake. Strain and add ice.
Garnish with orange slice.

BRITTANY

1½ oz. gin   1 tsp. orange juice
2 tsp. Amer Picon   orange twist
1 tsp. lemon juice

Combine with ice and shake. Strain and add ice. Garnish with fruit.

24

CARUSO

½ oz. gin   1 oz. dry vermouth
splash green crème de menthe

Serve over ice. Strain into a chilled cocktail glass.

CASINO

2 oz. gin   dash lemon juice
½ t. Maraschino   2 dashes orange bitters

Combine with ice and shake. Strain and add ice.

CHARLIE CHAPLIN

1½ oz. gin   1 oz. grenadine
2 oz. sweet & sour mix

Shake and serve.

CRISTIFORO COLUMBO

1½ oz. gin
½ oz. Campari
1 dash Blue Curaçao

club soda to fill
dash grenadine
4 oz. orange juice

Combine all but club soda and Curaçao with ice. Shake, strain and add ice. Fill with soda and float Blue Curaçao on top.

COCONUT GIN

1½ oz. gin
1 tsp. Maraschino

1 tsp. cream of coconut
2 tsp. lemon juice

Combine with ice and shake. Strain and add ice.

DEEP SEA

1 oz. gin
1 oz. dry vermouth
2 dashes Pernod

2 dashes orange bitters
1 olive
1 lemon twist

Combine with ice and shake. Strain and add ice. Garnish with fruit.

GIN FIZZ

1½ oz. gin   ½ juice of lemon
1 tsp. sugar   club soda to fill

*Shake well with cracked ice all but club soda. Strain into glass
over ice. Fill with club soda.*

GIN & TONIC

2 oz. gin   lime wedge
5 oz. tonic water

*Pour the ingredients in a highball glass with ice cube. Stir well.
Garnish with lime wedge.*

LONG ISLAND ICED TEA

½ oz. triple sec   ½ oz. tequila
½ oz. light rum   1 oz. sour mix
½ oz. gin   cola to fill
½ oz. vodka   lemon wedge

*Pour the spirits and sour mix into a collins glass with ice. Stir well
or shake. Top the glass off with cola. Garnish with the lemon wedge.*

CLUB MARTINI

1½ oz. gin   1 olive
2 tsp. sweet vermouth

Combine with ice and shake. Strain and serve straight up.
Garnish with olive.

MARTINI

2½ oz. gin   ½ oz. dry vermouth
1 green olive or lemon twist for garnish

Pour the ingredients into a cocktail shaker with ice cubes.   Stir well.
Strain into a chilled cocktail glass. Garnish with olive or lemon twist.

There are many variations on the classic martini:

- **Dry Martini** - Traditionally uses French vermouth, however recent trends define a Dry Martini as using little or no vermouth.
  - **Bone Dry or Desert Martini**- No vermouth.
  - **Gibson** - Garnish with a cocktail onion.
- **Perfect Martini** - Use equal parts of sweet and dry vermouth.
  - **Dirty Martini** - Add a small amount of olive brine.
  - **50–50** - Use equal parts of gin and dry vermouth.
- **Vodka Martini**- Replace gin with vodka for a nice alternative.

NAPOLEON

2 oz. gin   ½ oz. Dubonnet Rouge
½ oz. Grand Mariner

*Pour the ingredients into cocktail shaker with ice. Shake well.
Strain into a chilled cocktail glass.*

NEW ORLEANS FIZZ

1½ oz. gin   ¼ oz. cream
½ oz. lime juice   1 egg white*
½ oz. lemon juice   ¼ oz. club soda
½ oz. powdered sugar   3-4 dashes fleurs d'orange (orange flower water)

*Place all of the ingredients into a shaker with ice cubes. Shake
vigorously (more than normal to ensure the egg and cream are well
mixed). Strain into a chilled wine glass.*
Please use caution when using raw eggs as it may cause certain illnesses.

PICON CREMAILLERE

1½ oz gin   ¾ oz Dubonnet
¾ oz. Amer Picon   dash orange bitters

Stir with ice. Strain into a cocktail glass.

PINK LADY

1½ oz. gin
¼ oz. lemon juice
1-2 dashes grenadine

1 egg white*
maraschino cherry

*Pour the ingredients into a shaker with ice cubes. Shake well.
Strain into a chilled cocktail glass. Garnish with the cherry.
The egg white creates a "foam" that floats on top.*
Please use caution when using raw eggs as it may cause certain illnesses.

TOM COLLINS

1½ oz. gin
1 oz. lemon juice
½ oz. sugar syrup

club soda
maraschino cherry
lemon slice for garnish

*Pour the gin, lemon juice, and sugar syrup in a collins glass with ice cubes.
Stir thoroughly. Top with club soda. Garnish with cherry and lemon slice.*

TUXEDO

1½ oz. dry vermouth
1½ oz. gin
¼ tsp. maraschino liqueur

¼ tsp. anis liqueur
2 dashes bitters
maraschino cherry

*Pour all ingredients in a mixing glass filled with ice. Stir. Strain into
a chilled cocktail glass. Garnish with maraschino cherry.*

RUM

Rum is distilled from sugarcane by-products such as molasses and sugarcane juice. The process of fermentation and distillation produces the distillate, a clear liquid which is aged in oak and other casks. Rum production occurs mainly in the Caribbean and along the Demerara River in South America. Other popular rum producing locations include Australia and India.

Light rums with a clean taste are traditionally produced in Spanish speaking islands.

Darker rums from English speaking islands are rums with fuller taste containing greater amount of the molasses flavor and a caramel overtone.

Agricultural rums (rhum agricole) are produced in French speaking islands. These rums are made from sugar cane juice and are generally more expensive than molasses based rums.

Gold rums, or amber rums, are medium-bodied rums, which are generally aged. These gain their dark color from aging in wooden barrels, usually the charred white oak barrels that are the byproduct of Bourbon Whiskey.

Spiced rum obtains its flavor through addition of spices and caramel. Most are darker in color, and based on gold rums.

Overproof rums contain much higher than the standard 40% alcohol. Most of these rums bear greater than 75%, preparations of 151 to 160 proof.

Premium rums are very aged and carefully produced. They have more character and flavor than their "mixing" counterparts, and are generally consumed without the addition of other ingredients.

Cuba Libre, Mojito and Piña Colada are very famous rum drinks.

AROUND THE WORLD

1 dash rum
1 dash vodka
1 dash gin
1 dash tequila
1 dash triple sec
1 dash peach schnapps
1 dash Midori
1 dash Blue Curaçao
1 dash 151

1 dash Amaretto-Malibu
1 dash Chamord
1 dash sour mix
1 dash orange juice
1 dash pineapple juice
1 dash cranberry juice
1 dash lemon-lime soda

Fill glass with cracked ice. Add alcohol and even parts sour mix, orange, pineapple, and cranberry juices and lemon-lime soda. Shake. Serve in tall glass.

ARUBIAN KISS

1 oz. vodka
¾ oz. rum
¾ oz. banana liquor

2 dashes Blue Curaçao
1 oz. sour mix
3 oz. pineapple juice

Shake ingredients. Strain into a collins glass with ice.

BAHAMA MAMA

1½ oz. coconut rum
1½ oz. dark rum
splash orange juice
pineapple juice

dash grenadine
orange wedge
maraschino cherry

Shake over ice. Serve into a hurricane glass.
Garnish with an orange slice and maraschino cherry.

BANANA BARBADOS

¾ oz. Barbados rum
¾ oz. Jamaican rum
½ oz. crème de banana

splash of sour mix
2 scoops vanilla ice cream

Blend ingredients. Float a dash of rum.
Serve in hurricane glass.

BARBUDA BANANA MAN

1 oz. light rum
¼ oz. lemon juice or lime juice

½ tsp. sugar
1 banana

Blend with ice, serve in a cocktail glass. Garnish with banana slice.

BEACHCOMBER

1½ oz. rum
½ oz. triple sec
½ oz. lime juice

dash Maraschino liqueur
lime wedge

Shake with ice. Pour into a chilled cocktail glass with a sugared rim.
Garnish with a lime wedge.

BLACK ORCHID

1 oz. dark rum
1 oz. Chambord

½ oz. grenadine
½ oz. lemon-lime soda

Shake with ice. Strain into rocks glass. Top with lemon-lime soda.

BONAIRE BOOTY

1 oz. chocolate schnapps
¾ oz. Amaretto

½ oz. gold rum
1 oz. cream

Combine with ice and shake. Strain and serve over ice.

BLUE SKY

1½ oz. Canadian Mist
¾ oz. light rum
¾ oz. Blue Curaçao

8 oz. pineapple juice
orange wedge

*Blend all ingredients with ice until frozen. Use hurricane glass
and garnish with orange slice and umbrella.*

CAPTAIN'S COOLER

1 oz. spiced rum
½ oz. Grand Marnier
½ oz. triple sec
splash lemon-lime soda

½ oz. cranberry juice
1 oz. orange juice
½ oz. lime juice
lime wedge

*Combine all but soda and shake. Strain and add ice.
Fill with soda. Garnish with lime wedge.*

CARIBBEAN CRUISE

1 oz. spiced rum
1 oz. dark rum
¾ oz. coffee liqueur
¾ oz. cream of coconut

splash orange juice
splash pineapple juice
lemon twist

Blend with ice. Garnish with a lemon twist.

35

CALYPSO DAIQUIRI

1¼ oz. spiced rum
2½ oz. sour mix
½ oz. half & half

1 banana
1 tsp. vanilla extract

Blend with ice. Pour into daiquiri glass.

CAYMAN ISLAND RUM FREEZE

2 oz. rum
1 oz. triple sec
1 oz. grapefruit juice
2 oz. orange juice

½ oz. lime juice
½ cup ice cubes
orange wedge

Combine ingredients in blender. Blend until smooth. Pour into glass.
Garnish with orange wedge.

CONCH SHELL

4 oz. white rum
2 t. lime juice

½ cup ice

Combine with ice and shake. Strain and add ice.

CUBA LIBRE

1¼ oz. rum   dash lime juice
4 oz. cola   lime twist

Blend. Pour in glass over ice. Garnish with lime wedge.

DOMINICA BANANA DAIQUIRI

1½ oz. rum   ½ ripe banana (sliced)
½ oz. crème de banana   juice of 1 lime

*Blend all ingredients together until smooth
and pour unstrained into a tall chilled glass.*

HAVANA BANDANA

2 oz. rum   ½ oz. lime juice
3 dashes banana liqueur   3 oz. ice
1 banana

*Combine ingredients (except banana liqueur) and blend.
Float banana liqueur on top.*

HURRICANE

1 oz. rum
1 oz. dark rum
1 oz. apricot brandy

splash grenadine
2 tsp. lime juice
lime wedge

Shake with ice. Serve in hurricane glass. Garnish with lime wedge.

ISLAMORADA CHAMPAGNE COCKTAIL

1 oz. rum
3 oz. champagne
1 tsp. sugar

dash bitters
strawberry

In a tall glass mix rum, sugar and bitters. Fill with champagne.
Garnish with strawberry.

ISLE OF COCONUT

1½ oz. white rum
2 tsp. cream of coconut
2 tsp. lime juice
1 tsp. orange juice

½ tsp. sugar
1 tsp. lemon juice
coconut shavings

Mix all in blender with 3 oz. crushed ice until smooth.
Garnish with coconut.

JAMAICA GINGER

2 tsp. 151 rum
½ oz. Jamaican rum
1½ oz. white rum
2 tsp. Falernum
2 tsp. lime juice

1 tsp. white crème de menthe
1 slice pineapple
1 chunk ginger
splash ginger beer

*Combine rums, Falenum and juice with ice. Shake. Strain and add ice. Fill
with ginger beer. Dip pineapple in white crème de menthe.
Garnish with pineapple slice and ginger.*

KEY WEST

2 oz. rum
1 oz. grapefruit juice
juice of 1 lime

1 tsp. powdered sugar
dash of bitters
lime twist

Shake with ice. Strain into cocktail glass. Garnish with lime twist.

MAI TAI

2 oz. light rum
1 oz. triple sec
1 tsp. almond-flavored syrup
1 tsp. grenadine
1 tsp. lime juice

½ tsp. powdered sugar
pineapple wedge
maraschino cherry
dash of high-proof dark rum

*Shake with ice. Strain into tall glass about ¼ full with crushed ice. Top with a
dash of high-proof dark rum. Garnish with cherry and pineapple wedge.*

MARATHON SPARKLER

1 oz. spiced rum
1 oz. ruby red grapefruit juice
champagne

dash of grenadine
strawberry

*Fill glass with chilled champagne. Shake rum, grapefruit juice and
grenadine with ice. Strain into a champagne flute.
Garnish with strawberry on the rim.*

MARTINIQUE PUNCH

2 oz. rum
2 oz. mango
2 oz. orange juice

lime wedge
1 tsp. sugar
½ cup ice

Stir. Serve in rocks glass.

MIAMI RUM YUM

1 oz. Bailey's Irish Cream
1 oz. rum

1 oz. cream

Blend with ice. Pour in chilled cocktail glass.

MOJITO

2 oz. white rum
splash of club soda

½ tsp. powdered sugar
mint leaves

Muddle mint leaves with powdered sugar. Add ice, rum and top with club soda. Garnish with a sprig of fresh mint.

PIÑA COLADA

2 oz light rum
3 Tbsp. cream of coconut

3 Tbsp. pineapple juice

Shake with ice. Serve in hurricane glass. Or blend with ice cream for frozen variation. Garnish with fresh pineapple wedge. Top with whipped cream if frozen.

PUERTO RICAN RUMBALL

1 oz. rum
¾ oz. Midori

splash orange juice

Shake with ice. Strain into chilled cocktail glass.

TROPICAL STORM

1 oz. light rum
½ oz. banana liqueur
2 oz. orange juice
1 splash grenadine

1 splash pineapple juice
1 sliced banana
½ cup crushed ice

Blend until smooth. Pour into hurricane glass.

VIRGIN ISLANDS RUM RUNNER

1 oz. rum
½ oz. blackberry brandy
1 oz. crème de banana
splash pineapple juice

splash orange juice
dash grenadine
dash dark rum

Shake. Serve on the rocks in highball glass.
Float a bit of dark rum on top.

YO HO HO AND A BARREL OF RUM

1½ oz. old-fashioned root beer
1 oz. rum

1 oz. milk or cream

Combine in blender with ice until smooth. Pour into a cocktail glass.

TEQUILA

Tequila is a spirit made from the blue agave plant, produced in the area surrounding Tequila, a town in the western Mexican state of Jalisco. Tequila is most often made at a 38% - 40% alcohol content (76 - 80 proof), but there are also other varieties of Tequila produced with 43% - 46% alcohol content (86 - 92 proof).

The five categories of tequila are:
- **Oro** ("gold") unaged tequila, "joven y abogado" (young and adulterated) caramel, fructose, glycerin and wood flavoring can be added to resemble aged tequila.
- **Blanco** ("white") or plata ("silver") not aged white spirit.
- **Reposado** ("rested") aged a minimum of 2 months but less than a year in oak barrels.
- **Añejo** ("aged" or "vintage") aged minimum 1 year but less than 3 years in oak barrels.
- **Extra añejo** ("extra aged") or ultra aged– aged minimum 3 years in oak barrels.

Aztec, Margarita and Tequila Sunrise are well known tequila drinks.

ACAPULCO

1½ oz. tequila
½ oz. light rum
½ oz. triple sec

1 oz. sour mix
splash lime juice
fresh mint leaves

Shake with ice and strain into an ice filled double old-fashioned glass.
Garnish with mint leaves.

AZTEC

1½ oz. tequila
1 oz. coffee liqueur

1 oz. white crème de cacao
1½ dashes Blue Curaçao

Shake with cracked ice and strain.
Pour into chilled cocktail glass.

BAJA GOLD

2 oz. añejo tequila
½ oz. triple sec
3½ oz. pineapple juice

juice of 1 lime
sugar to taste
lime wedge

Pour the ingredients into a shaker with ice cubes. Shake well. Strain
into a half-sized cocktail glass. Garnish with lime wedge.

BANANA MARGARITA

2 oz. tequila
½ oz. crème de banana
2 oz. sour mix

½ banana
1½ cups ice
lime wedge

*Combine with crushed ice until smooth. Pour into sugar
rimmed glass. Garnish with lime wedge.*

BLOODY MARIA

1½ oz. tequila
dash Worcestershire
dash Tabasco
dash salt
dash pepper

½ lime
tomato juice to fill
celery stalk
lime wedge

*Build in exact order in a tall glass.
Garnish with celery stalk and lime wedge.*

BLUE LAGOON MARGARITA

1¼ oz. tequila
¾ oz. Blue Curaçao
1 tsp. lime juice

splash lemon-lime soda
pineapple juice to fill
pineapple wedge

Shake. Pour over ice. Garnish with pineapple wedge.

BLUE MONDAYS

1 oz. tequila
1 oz. Cointreau
1 oz. Midori

1 oz. lemon juice
2 kiwi fruits peeled
kiwi wedge

Frost the rim of goblet with salt. Combine ingredients in blender with ice. Blend until smooth. Garnish with kiwi wedge.

BLUE SHARK

1½ oz. tequila
1½ oz. vodka

½ oz. Blue Curaçao
lime slice

Combine with ice and shake. Strain and add ice. Garnish with lime slice.

BRAHMA BULL

1½ oz. tequila

½ oz. coffee liqueur

Combine with ice and stir.

CHAPALA

1½ oz. tequila
2 tsp. grenadine
2 tsp. lemon juice

2 tsp. orange juice
orange slice

*Combine with ice and shake. Strain and add ice.
Garnish with fruit.*

CHIHUAHUA

1 oz. tequila
2 dashes bitters

3 oz. grapefruit juice
lime wedge

Combine with ice and stir. Garnish with lemon wedge.

COCONUT TEQUILA

1½ oz. tequila
1 tsp. Maraschino
2 tsp. cream of coconut

2 tsp. lemon juice
4 oz. ice

Combine with crushed ice and blend until smooth.

CONCHITA

1½ oz. tequila   1 dash lemon juice
1 oz. grapefruit juice

Combine with ice and shake. Strain and add ice.

CUCARACHA

2 oz. tequila   1 oz. coffee liqueur

*Mix in a cocktail glass. Light on fire for one minute and drink
with a straw while burning.*

DAGGER

½ oz. tequila   ½ oz. peppermint schnapps
½ oz. dark crème de cacao

Layer in shot glass.

DULCE DE TEQUILA

2 oz. Tequila Tezón Reposado
1 oz. Cognac
1 oz. Cointreau
½ oz. lime juice

1 tsp. agave nectar
large-grained sugar for rimming
lemon wedge

*Pour the ingredients into a cocktail shaker with ice. Shake well. Strain into
a chilled cocktail glass rimmed with sugar. Garnish with lemon wedge.*

EARTHQUAKE

1½ oz. tequila
1 tsp. grenadine
1 quart strawberry

2 dashes orange bitters
1 lime wedge
3 oz. ice

Blend until smooth. Garnish with lime wedge.

GOLDEN MARGARITA

1½ oz. gold tequila
½ oz. triple sec
½ oz. lime juice
3 oz. sour mix

dash orange juice
lime wedge
salt for rimming glass (optional)

*Pour the ingredients into a shaker with ice cubes. Shake well.
If desired, salt the rim of a chilled cocktail glass. Pour contents,
with ice, into the glass. Garnish with lime wedge.*

GREEN IGUANA

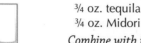

¾ oz. tequila 3 oz. sour mix
¾ oz. Midori

Combine with ice and shake well. Strain and add ice.
Garnish with fruit.

HAWAIIAN MARGARITA

1½ oz. tequila dash of sour mix
½ oz. triple sec 1 cup of ice
2 oz. fresh or frozen strawberries strawberry
2 oz. fresh or canned pineapple pineapple wedge

Pour the ingredients into a blender. Blend until smooth.
Pour contents into a chilled cocktail glass. Garnish with
strawberry and pineapple wedge.

ICEBREAKER

2 oz. tequila 1 Tbsp. grenadine
2 tsp. Cointreau 4 oz. ice
2 oz. grapefruit juice

Combine with crushed ice. Blend until smooth.

KEY WEST MARGARITA

1½ oz. tequila
1 oz. melon liqueur
½ oz. crème of coconut
½ oz. pineapple juice

½ oz. lime juice
½ oz. orange juice
1 dash grenadine
½ cup crushed ice

Blend until smooth. Pour into a hurricane glass.

LONG BEACH

¾ oz tequila
¾ oz. rum
¾ oz. gin
¾ oz. vodka

¾ oz. triple sec
splash sour mix
splash cranberry juice
lemon wedge

Shake all. Pour in hurricane glass. Garnish with lemon wedge.

MARGARITA

1½ oz. tequila
½ oz. triple sec
dash of lemon or lime juice

3 oz. sour mix
lime wedge
salt to rim the glass (optional)

Pour the ingredients into a shaker with ice cubes. Shake well.
If desired, salt the rim of a chilled margarita glass.
Pour contents, with ice, into the glass. Garnish with lime wedge.

MEXI-TINI

1 oz. tequila
1 oz. orange flavored vodka

½ oz. orange juice
orange slice

*Pour ingredients into cocktail shaker and add crushed ice. Let stand
for five seconds. Shake vigorously for five seconds.
Strain into martini glass and garnish with orange slice.*

PALOMA

2 oz. blanco or reposado tequila
6 oz. fresh grapefruit juice
½ oz. lime juice

splash club soda
salt for rimming

*Rim cocktail glass with salt. Fill the glass with ice and add the tequila,
grapefruit juice and lime juice. Add a splash of soda.*

PASSION COCTAIL

2 oz. gold tequila
3 oz. cranberry juice
1 oz. lime juice

2 oz. Grand Marnier
lime slice

*Pour tequila, cranberry juice, and lime juice into a shaker with ice
cubes. Shake well. Strain into a chilled stemmed glass.
Splash with Grand Marnier. Garnish with lime slice.*

PEACH MARGARITA

1½ oz. tequila   ¼ oz. lime juice
¼ oz. triple sec   1 cup ice
¼ oz. peach schnapps
1 skinned, pitted, fresh medium peach or equivalent canned peaches

Pour the ingredients into a blender. Blend until smooth. Pour the contents into a chilled cocktail glass.

RASPBERRY MARGARITA

1½ oz. tequila   ½ cup raspberries (frozen)
1 oz. triple sec   ½ cup ice
1 oz. lime juice   fresh raspberries for garnish

Combine ½ cup ice with ingredients. Blend until frothy.

TEQUILA FUEGO

1½ oz. premium tequila   1 jalapeno ring
½ tsp. hot sauce   kosher salt
juice of one lime wedge   1 lime wedge

Use lime wedge to moisten ½ the brim of the shooter glass. Dip the moistened brim in salt. In a small glass, mix the lime juice, tequila and hot sauce. Place the jalapeno ring in the bottom of the shooter glass and top with tequila mixture. Optional- Follow the shot with a lime wedge.

TEQUILA SUNRISE

4 oz. orange juice
2 oz. tequila
½ oz. grenadine

orange slice
maraschino cherry

Pour tequila and orange juice into highball glass with ice cubes. Stir.
Carefully top the drink with the grenadine.
Garnish with orange slice and cherry.

TEZÓN CARAMEL APPLE PIE

1 oz. Tezón Tequila
½ oz. butterscotch schnapps
1 oz. apple cider

1 tsp. fresh lemon juice
apple slice

Pour the ingredients into a cocktail shaker filled with ice. Shake well.
Strain into a chilled cocktail glass. Garnish with apple slice.

ZIPPER

½ oz. Grand Marnier
½ oz. tequila

½ oz. Irish cream

Layer in shot glass.

VODKA

Vodka is a distilled beverage which is typically colorless, containing ethanol purified by distillation from fermented grain or molasses. It usually has an alcohol content ranging from 35% to 50% by volume. The classic Russian and Polish vodka is 40% (USA 80 proof). Vodka today is one of the world's most popular spirits. Its popularity is in part to its reputation as an alcoholic beverage for detecting no smell of liquor on the breath.

In Eastern Europe and Scandinavia vodka is generally drunk neat. In many other countries vodka is used in cocktails and other mixed drinks, such as the Bloody Mary, Screwdriver and Vodka Tonic.

Vodka may be distilled from any starch-rich plant matter; most vodka today is produced from grains such as sorghum, corn, wheat or rye. Rye and wheat vodkas are typically considered superior. Vodka is also made from potatoes, molasses, soybeans, grapes and sugar beets. In Poland some vodka is produced by just fermenting a solution of crystal sugar and yeast.

Bloody Mary, Cosmopolitan and Screwdriver are world famous vodka drinks.

ABSOLUTELY CRUSHED

2 oz. lemon flavored vodka   2 whole passion fruits
2 oz. Passoa   2 cups crushed ice
4 whole kumquats   1 Tbsp. raw sugar

*Slice passion fruit and put seeds in a highball glass. Slice kumquats
and crush together with sugar and passion fruit. Add crushed ice.
Pour lemon flavored vodka over ice and stir.
Add more crushed ice. Pour Passoa.*

APPLE PUCKER

1 oz. vodka   dash lemon lime soda
1 oz. Green Apple Pucker   1 slice lemon

*Combine all in shaker over ice.
Mix and pour into chilled highball glass.*

BAILEY'S COMET

¾ oz. Irish cream   splash club soda
½ oz. dark crème de cacao   splash cream
½ oz. vodka

Combine with ice and shake. Strain and serve straight up.

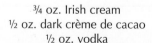

BLACK RUSSIAN

1½ oz. vodka   ¾ oz. coffee liqueur

Pour over ice in a rocks glass.

BLOODY BULL

1 oz. vodka   lime wedge
2½ oz. Bull Shot   maraschino cherry

Combine with ice and stir.
Garnish with lime and maraschino cherry.

BLOODY MARY

1½ oz. vodka   ground pepper
3 oz. tomato juice   hot pepper sauce
½ oz. lemon juice   celery stalk
dash of Worcestershire sauce   lemon and/or lime wedge
celery salt

Build liquid ingredients in highball glass over ice cubes. Mix well.
Add the seasonings to taste. Garnish with lemon
and/or lime wedge and celery stalk.

BLUE MAX

1 oz. vodka
½ oz. Blue Curaçao
2 oz. cream of coconut

2 oz. cream
3 oz. pineapple juice
orange slice

Combine with ice and blend. Garnish with orange slice.

BRAIN ERASER

1 oz. vodka
½ oz. coffee liqueur

½ oz. Amaretto
splash club soda

Combine with ice and stir.

BUBBLE GUM

½ oz. crème de banana
½ oz. Midori
½ oz. vodka
¼ oz. grenadine

½ oz. orange juice
½ oz. sour mix
orange twist

*Combine with ice and shake. Strain and serve straight up.
Garnish with orange twist.*

BULL WITCH PROJECT

1 oz. black vodka
1 oz. spiced rum
splash cranberry juice

splash pineapple juice
splash Red Bull
cinnamon sticks

Shake all ingredients and strain into a martini glass. Garnish with cinnamon sticks arranged like the Blair Witch Trees.

CHI CHI

1 oz. vodka
splash crème of coconut
pineapple juice

dash cream
pineapple wedge

Blend with crushed ice. Garnish with pineapple wedge.

CHIQUITA

1½ oz. vodka
2 tsp. banana liqueur
2 t. lime juice

1 tsp. sugar
2 oz. banana
3 oz. ice

Combine with crushed ice and blend until smooth.

CHOCOLATE BLACK RUSSIAN

1 oz. coffee liqueur   2 scoops chocolate ice cream
½ oz. vodka   maraschino cherry

Mix in blender until smooth. Garnish with maraschino cherry.

CHOCOLATE & ORANGE MARTINI

1 oz. vodka   dash of Cointreau or Grand Marnier
½ oz. white crème de cacao   chunks of chocolate for rimming

Pour vodka and crème de cacao into a cocktail shaker half-filled with ice. Add dash of Cointreau or Grand Marnier. Shake well. Strain into the prepared glass.

To make the chocolate rim:
Place chunks of chocolate into a heat-safe bowl. Place this bowl over a pot of water. Heat and simmer the water until the chocolate is completely melted. Pour the melted chocolate onto a plate and dip the rim of the cocktail glass into the chocolate. Stand the glass upright. Allow the chocolate to set. Chill the glass.

COSMOPOLITAN

1½ oz. vodka   3 oz. cranberry juice
1 oz. Cointreau   1 oz. lemon juice

Mix with ice in a shaker. Put into a cocktail glass and garnish with a slice of lime.

CREAMY SCREWDRIVER

2 oz. vodka
1 egg yolk*
4 oz. orange juice

1 tsp. sugar syrup
4 oz. ice

Combine with crushed ice. Blend until smooth.
Please use caution when using raw eggs as it may cause certain illnesses.

CROCODILE COOLER

1 oz. vodka
1 oz. Midori

splash sour mix
splash lemon lime soda

Shake all but lemon lime soda. Pour into a tall glass.
Top with soda.

CURAÇAO COOLER

1 oz. Blue Curaçao
1 oz. vodka
2 tsp. lemon juice

2 tsp. lime juice
orange juice to fill
lemon twist

Combine with ice and shake. Strain and add ice.
Garnish with fruit.

DAISY PUSHER

½ oz. vodka
½ oz. gin
½ oz rum

¼ oz. tequila
1 shot Irish cream
lime twist

*Hand swirl in glass. Pour over rocks in a pony glass
with a lime twist.*

DEATH BY CHOCOLATE

1 oz. vodka
1 oz. chocolate syrup
1 oz. coffee liqueur
1 oz. dark crème de cacao

2 scoops chocolate ice cream
whipped cream for topping
1 cup crushed ice
maraschino cherry

*Pour all the ingredients into a blender. Blend until smooth.
Pour into a stemmed glass. Top with whipped cream.
Garnish with maraschino cherry.*

DIRTY ASHTRAY

½ oz. vodka
½ oz. gin
½ oz. light rum
½ oz. tequila
½ oz. Blue Curaçao

½ oz. grenadine
splash pineapple juice
splash sour mix
lemon wedge

Shake. Strain into chilled cocktail glass. Garnish with lemon wedge.

ELECTRIC LEMONADE

1½ oz. vodka
½ oz. Blue Curaçao
2 oz. sweet & sour mix

splash lemon-lime soda
lemon slice

Blend until smooth. Garnish with lemon slice.

FUZZY NAVEL

1 oz. vodka
1 oz. peach liqueur

3 oz. orange juice
peach wedge

Pour the ingredients into a cocktail glass with ice cubes.
Stir well. Garnish with peach wedge.

HARVEY WALLBANGER

¾ oz. vodka
1½ oz. orange juice
¼ oz. Galliano

orange slice
maraschino cherry

Pour vodka and orange juice into cocktail glass with ice cubes.
Add the Galliano. Garnish with orange slice
and maraschino cherry.

KEY LIME PIE MARTINI

2 oz. vanilla vodka
½ oz. triple sec
2½ oz. pineapple juice

½ oz. lime cordial
½ lime
crushed graham crackers for rimming

Rim a chilled cocktail glass with finely crushed graham crackers. Pour vodka, triple sec, pineapple juice and lime cordial into a cocktail shaker with ice. Squeeze the juice from the lime into the shaker. Shake well. Strain into cocktail glass.

LEMON DROP

1½ oz. vodka
splash sour mix

dash lemon juice
lemon wedge

Shake. Strain into chilled sugar rimmed cocktail glass. Garnish with lemon wedge.

LIFESAVER

1 oz. vodka
1 oz. triple sec
2 oz. orange juice

2 oz. pineapple juice
1/2 tsp. grenadine
pineapple wedge

Blend and pour over ice. Garnish with pineapple wedge.

LOVE POTION #9

1 oz. strawberry, vanilla or clear vodka
½ oz. white crème de cacao
½ cup fresh or frozen strawberries

scoop of vanilla ice cream
½ cup ice
strawberry for garnish

Pour the ingredients into a blender. Blend until smooth. Pour into a chilled cocktail glass. Garnish with strawberry. If the mix is too thick, add berries or milk; too thin, add ice or ice cream.

SCREWDRIVER

2 oz. vodka

5 oz. orange juice

Build ingredients in a cocktail glass with ice. Stir well.

SEA BREEZE

1¾ oz. vodka
3 oz. cranberry juice

1 oz. grapefruit juice
grapefruit slice for garnish

Pour the vodka and cranberry juice into cocktail glass with ice cubes. Stir well. Top off with the grapefruit juice. Garnish with grapefruit slice.

SEX ON THE BEACH

1½ oz. vodka
¾ oz. peach schnapps
½ oz. crème de cassis
2 oz. orange juice

2 oz. cranberry juice
orange slice
maraschino cherry

Pour all the ingredients into a shaker with ice cubes. Shake well. Strain into cocktail glass. Garnish with orange slice and maraschino cherry.

VODKA COLLINS

2 oz. vodka
sour mix to fill
splash club soda water

orange slice
maraschino cherry

Pour the vodka into a cocktail glass filled with ice. Fill with sour mix. Shake well. Add a splash of club soda. Garnish with cherry and orange slice.

Replace the vodka with gin for a Tom Collins or bourbon for a John Collins.

WHITE SANDS

1 oz. vodka
½ oz. coconut rum
splash triple sec

1 scoop vanilla ice cream
1 cup crushed ice

Blend until smooth. Pour into a collins glass.

WHISKEY

Whiskey refers to a broad category of alcoholic beverages that are distilled from fermented grain mash and aged in oak casks. Barley, malted barley, rye, malted rye, corn and wheat are varieties of grains used to produce whiskey.

Scotch whiskies are generally distilled twice, while some are distilled a third time and matured for a minimum of three years in oak casks.

American whiskey is aged in oak casks for at least two years. All straight whiskeys except straight corn whiskey must be aged in new casks that have been charred on the inside surface. American blended whiskeys combine straight whiskey with un-aged whiskey, grain neutral spirits, flavorings and colorings.

Mint Julep, Old Fashioned and Whiskey Sour are some of the most popular mixed drinks made with whiskey.

ADMIRAL HIGHBALL

1½ oz. bourbon
1½ oz. Tokay wine
1 dash lemon juice

dash pineapple juice
dash lime-lime soda

Mix in a highball glass. Add ice and fill with lemon lime soda.

AFFINITY COCKTAIL

1 oz. whiskey
1 oz. dry sherry

1 oz. sweet vermouth
2 dashes angostura bitters

*Blend ingredients. Serve over cracked ice
or strain to serve straight up.*

AMERICANA

1 tsp. bourbon
1 dash angostura bitters

4 oz. champagne
slice peach

*Pour the bourbon and bitters into a flute. Add champagne.
Garnish with the peach slice.*

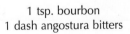

ANGELIC

1 oz. bourbon
½ oz. white crème de cacao

dash grenadine
2 oz. half & half

Shake with ice and serve on rocks or stain into cocktail glass.

AQUARIUS

1½ oz. blended whiskey
½ oz. cherry brandy

1 oz. cranberry juice

Build over ice in a lowball glass.

BABY'S BOTTOM

1½ oz. whiskey
½ oz. white crème de cacao

½ oz. white crème de menthe

Stir over ice. Strain into chilled cocktail glass.

BLUE BELL

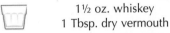

1½ oz. whiskey
1 Tbsp. dry vermouth

2 dashes bitters

Combine with ice and shake. Strain and add ice.

BOBBY BURNS

1½ oz. whiskey
½ oz. Drambuie

½ oz. sweet vermouth

Combine with ice and stir. Strain and serve straight up.

BOURBON CARDINAL

1½ oz. bourbon
1 dash maraschino juice
1 Tbsp. cranberry juice
1 Tbsp. grapefruit juice

2 tsp. lemon juice
1 tsp. sugar
2 maraschino cherries

Combine with ice and shake. Strain and serve straight up.
Garnish with cherries.

BOURBON COLLINS

2 oz. bourbon
splash club soda
1 slice lemon

½ oz. lemon juice
2 dashes bitters
1 Tbsp. sugar syrup

Combine all but soda with ice and shake well.
Strain and add soda and ice. Garnish with fruit.

BOURBON FLIP

2 oz. bourbon
1 egg*
1 splash cream

½ splash sugar syrup
1 dash nutmeg

Combine with ice and shake. Strain and serve straight up.
*Please use caution when using raw eggs as it may cause certain illnesses.

BOURBON PUNCH

1 quart bourbon
1 quart club soda
4 oz. grenadine
3 slices lemon

3 slices orange
6 oz. orange juice
3 oz. sugar
3 oz. lemon juice

Combine with ice and stir. Serves 8.

CALIFORNIA LEMONADE

2 oz. whiskey
1 dash grenadine

2 oz. sour mix

Shake and strain. Add ice and serve into cocktail glass.

CARIBBEAN JOY

1½ oz. whiskey
2 dashes Cointreau

2 tsp. lime juice
1 tsp. powdered sugar

Combine with ice and shake. Strain and add ice.

CHAPEL HILL

1½ oz. bourbon
½ oz. triple sec

1 Tbsp. lemon juice
orange twist

Combine with ice and shake. Strain and serve straight up.
Garnish with orange twist.

COASTAL KISS

1 oz. whiskey
1 oz. Amaretto

6 oz. pineapple juice

Mix in blender with ice until smooth.

COLUMBIA SKIN

9 oz. Scotch
1 lemon peel

6 slices lemon
2 cups water

Combine with boiling water and stir.
Serve hot and top with lemon slices.

COMFORTABLE COLADA

1½ oz. whiskey
1 oz. cream of coconut
2 oz. pineapple juice

2 cups crushed ice
2 maraschino cherries

Blend until smooth. Serve in tall glasses over ice.
Garnish with cherries.

73

DOWN UNDER

1 oz. whiskey
1 oz. Irish cream

1 oz. coffee liqueur
splash cream

Build over ice in a snifter.

DRY MANHATTAN COOLER

2 oz. whiskey
1 oz. dry vermouth
2 tsp. lemon juice

2 oz. orange juice
2 tsp. almond extract
club soda to fill

Combine all but club soda with ice.
Shake, strain and add soda with ice.

ELECTRIC KOOL AID

½ oz. whiskey
½ oz. Amaretto
½ oz. cherry brandy
½ oz. Midori

½ oz. triple sec
½ oz. cranberry juice
½ oz. sour mix
2 dashes grenadine

Combine with ice and shake. Strain and serve straight up.

GREAT LADY

¾ oz. bourbon
1 oz. coffee liqueur
2 oz. milk

½ oz. honey
1 dash cinnamon
1 maraschino cherry

Mix in blender with ice until smooth.
Garnish with cinnamon and cherry.

HAWAIIAN SNOW

1 oz. bourbon
1 oz. coffee liqueur
5 oz. milk

4 oz. ice
1 small orchid

Combine with crushed ice and blend until smooth.
Garnish with orchid.

HOT TODDY

1 oz. brandy or blended whiskey
1 Tbsp. honey
¼ lemon

1 cup hot water
1 tea bag

Coat the bottom of a mug the honey. Add brandy and juice of the lemon
quarter. On the side, heat water in a teakettle and add tea bag to make
hot tea. Pour the steaming tea into honey/brandy/lemon combination.

HUNTER'S COCKTAIL

1½ oz. whiskey
½ oz. cherry brandy

maraschino cherry

*Pour whiskey and cherry brandy into
a cocktail glass with ice. Stir well.*

KENTUCKY COLONEL

1½ oz. bourbon
½ oz. Benedictine

lemon twist

*Shake with ice. Strain into chilled cocktail glass.
Garnish with lemon twist.*

MINT JULEP

4 oz. bourbon
4-6 mint leaves

2 sugar cubes
mint sprig

*Place the ingredients into a cocktail shaker. Muddle well to dissolve
the sugar and to release the oil and aroma of the mint. Add ice cubes
to the shaker. Shake well. Strain into a julep cup or collins glass with
ice cubes. Garnish with the mint sprig.*

MANHATTAN

1¼ oz. rye whiskey
½ oz. sweet vermouth

2-3 dashes Angostura bitters
maraschino cherry

*Pour the ingredients into a mixing glass with ice cubes. Stir well.
Strain into a chilled cocktail glass. Garnish with maraschino cherry.*

Variations on the Manhattan:

• **Dry Manhattan** - Use a dash of dry vermouth and garnish with a lemon twist.
• **Perfect Manhattan**- Equal parts of sweet and dry vermouth. Garnish with a lemon twist.
• **Brandy Manhattan** - Replace whiskey with brandy.
• **Scotch Manhattan** - Replace whiskey with Scotch.
• **Southern Comfort Manhattan** - Replace whiskey with Southern Comfort.

OLD-FASHIONED

2 oz. bourbon
2-3 dashes Angostura bitters
2 orange slices

½ oz. club soda
1 sugar cube
maraschino cherry

*Place sugar cube at bottom of cocktail glass. Saturate the cube with
bitters. Add one orange slice. Muddle these ingredients. Fill the
glass with ice cubes. Add bourbon and club soda. Stir well. Garnish
with a second orange slice and maraschino cherry.*

WIDOW NIGHTCAP

2 oz. scotch   4 oz. milk
½ oz. dark crème de cacao

Shake with ice. Strain into chilled cocktail glass.

WHISKEY SOUR

1½ oz. bourbon   ¾ oz. sugar syrup
1½ oz. lemon juice   maraschino cherry

*Pour the bourbon, lemon juice, and sugar syrup into a shaker with ice
cubes. Shake well. Strain into a chilled cocktail glass.
Garnish with the cherry.*

WHITE CHRISTMAS

1 oz. whiskey   ½ oz. white chocolate liqueur
4 oz. eggnog   edible gold flakes or chocolate flakes

*Pour the ingredients in snifter.
Sprinkle gold or chocolate flakes on top.*

INDEX

79

INDEX